Chefs' Special

Vegetarian Fiesta

Vegetarian Fiesta

Chefs' Special

Compiled by
Master Chefs
of India

Lustre Press
Roli Books

GOURMET DELIGHT

n a land so rich in cultural heritage, it is but natural that the Indian cuisine is multifarious, offering a delight to both the eye and the palate. Its myriad flavours and cooking traditions find their roots in its historical influences. The Mughals revolutionised the art of Indian cooking with their delectable *biryanis* (an exquisite oven preparation with meat/vegetables, herbs and seasonings), *kormas* (a spicy meat or vegetarian preparation), *kebabs* and *tikkas* (meat and vegetables cooked in small pieces, usually on skewers) made in a *tandoor* (an oven made of mud and heated by a slow charcoal fire). The British Raj spawned an interesting Anglo-Indian gastronomic culture which is still eaten with relish. Different regions in India offer their own specialities with their very own taste, subtlety and aroma. The country's vast reservoir of spices made from its abundance of tropical herbs, serves as garnishing and contains medicinal and preservative properties. Indeed the range of the Indian cuisine can amaze even a connoisseur.

Vegetarian Fiesta offers you an assortment of snacks, dry preparations and curries. From the popular 'potato' to the vegetarian's meat—'cottage cheese', try your hand at different cooking styles. A few basic recipes of popular cooking ingredients, Indian equivalents of foods given in each list of ingredients and a Glossary of Cooking Terms are valuable add-ons. A multi-purpose chutney, mixed pickle and relishing *rotis* (pp. 86-91) serve as a complementary fillip. And to provide a finishing touch, a sprinkling of 'handy hints' are added as sure-fire remedies to common culinary problems.

5

BASIC INDIAN RECIPES

Green Chilli Paste
Chop the required quantity of green chillies and process until pulped.

Garam Masala (for 450 gm)
Put 200 gm cumin, 35 gm peppercorns, 45 gm black cardamoms, 30 gm green cardamoms, 60 gm coriander seeds, 20 gm cloves, 20 gm cinnamon sticks, 15 gm bayleaves and 2 nutmegs in a processor and grind to a fine powder. Transfer to a bowl, add 20 gm mace powder and 30 gm ginger powder and mix well. Sieve and store in an airtight container.

Brown Onion Paste
Fry sliced onions over medium heat till brown. Drain excess oil and allow to cool. Process until pulped, (using very little water if required). Refrigerate in an airtight container.

Yoghurt
Boil milk and keep aside till lukewarm. Add 2 tsp yoghurt to the milk and mix well. Allow to ferment for 6-8 hours.

Red Chilli Paste
Chop red chillies and process until pulped.

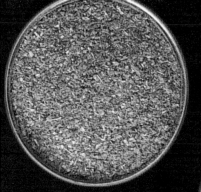

Garam Masala

Green Chilli
Paste

Yoghurt

Brown Onion Paste

Red Chilli Paste

Ginger/Garlic Paste
Soak ginger/garlic overnight. Peel, chop and process to pulp. Refrigerate in an airtight container.

Onion Paste
Peel and quarter onions and process until pulped. Refrigerate in an airtight container.

Tomato Purée
Peel, deseed and chop the tomatoes. Transfer to a pan, add 1 lt water, 8 cloves, 8 green cardamoms, 15 gm ginger, 10 gm garlic, 5 bayleaves and 5 peppercorns and cook on medium heat till the tomatoes are tender. Cool and process to a pulp.

Cottage Cheese (*Paneer*)
Heat 3 lt milk. Just before it boils, add 60 ml/4 tsp lemon juice or white vinegar. Strain the milk through a muslin cloth and hang for 2-3 hours to drain the whey and moisture.

Khoya
Boil milk in a wok (*kadhai*). Reduce heat and cook, stirring occasionally, till the quantity is reduced to half. Then stir constantly and scrape from all sides till a thick paste-like consistency is obtained. Allow to cool. *Khoya* is also called wholemilk fudge.

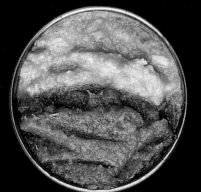
Ginger-Garlic Paste

Cottage Cheese

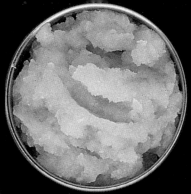
Onion Paste

Tomato Puree

Khoya

POTATO BASKETS

Serves: 4-6   Preparation time: 5-6 minutes   Cooking time: 20 minutes

Ingredients

Potatoes (large), boiled, peeled *8*
Chickpeas *(kabuli chana)*, boiled
150 gm / ¾ cup
Chaat masala *15 gm / 1 tbsp*
Ginger *(adrak)*, finely chopped
15 gm / 1 tbsp
Green chillies, finely chopped
10 gm / 2 tsp
Green coriander *(hara dhaniya)*,
finely chopped *15 gm / 1 tbsp*
Lemon juice *30 ml / 2 tbsp*
Salt to taste

Method

1. Cut the potatoes in half and carefully scoop out the centres.
2. Mix together the boiled chickpeas, chaat masala, chopped ginger, green chillies, green coriander, lemon juice and salt.
3. Fill the mixture into the centre of the scooped potatoes. Arrange on a flat dish and serve.

BATTER-COATED STUFFED TOMATOES

Serves: 6   Preparation time: 30-40 minutes   Cooking time: 30-40 minutes

Ingredients

Tomatoes *350-450 gm*
Cottage cheese *(paneer)* (p. 8)
140 gm / $^3/_5$ cup
Black pepper *(kali mirch)*, ground
1 gm / $^1/_4$ tsp
Asafoetida *(hing)* powder *1 gm / $^1/_4$ tsp*
Green coriander *(hara dhaniya)*,
chopped *30 gm / 2 tbsp*
Oil for frying
For the batter:
Gram flour *(besan)*, sifted
60 gm / 4 tbsp
Cayenne pepper *(Kashmiri lal mirch)*
1 gm / $^1/_4$ tsp
Salt *1 gm / $^1/_4$ tsp*
Baking powder *1 gm / $^1/_4$ tsp*
Water, cold *50 ml / $^1/_4$ cup*

Method

1. Slice stems off the tomatoes and hollow out the centres; drain upside down on a paper towel.
2. Knead cottage cheese and spices together. Fill each tomato cup with the mixture.
3. Mix the ingredients for the batter, adding water slowly. Whisk until the batter is smooth and thick enough to seal in the filling and to evenly coat the tomatoes.
4. Dip each filled tomato in the batter, coating evenly. Deep fry until golden brown on all sides. Remove, drain on paper towels. Serve hot.

CRISPY BENGAL GRAM STRIPS

Serves: 4-6   Preparation time: 5-6 hours   Cooking time: 30 minutes

Ingredients

Bengal gram *(chana dal)*
200 gm / 1 cup
Coriander *(dhaniya)* seeds
15 gm / 1 tbsp
Peppercorns *(kali mirch)*
15 gm / 1 tbsp
Ginger *(adrak)*, chopped *10 gm / 2 tsp*
Green coriander *(hara dhaniya)*,
chopped *15 gm /1 tbsp*
Green chillies, chopped *2*
Salt to taste
Red chilli powder *5 gm / 1 tsp*
Garam masala (p. 6) *5 gm / 1 tsp*
Oil for frying

Method

1. Soak Bengal gram for 4-5 hours or in warm water for half an hour. Drain and blend along with coriander seeds and peppercorns to make a coarsely ground thick paste.
2. Put the paste into a big bowl with the remaining ingredients. Mix thoroughly, keep for 30 minutes.
3. Heat oil in a wok *(kadhai)* till it starts smoking. Moisten hands and shape the mixture into 10-cm flat patties. Fry patties for 2-3 minutes on both sides and remove from oil. Drain excess oil and allow to cool.
4. Slice the patties into 3-4 strips. Reheat oil till it starts smoking. Lower heat to medium and fry the strips till they are crisp and golden brown on both sides. Drain excess oil and serve hot.

TANDOORI COTTAGE CHEESE SALAD

Serves: 4-5   Preparation time: 2 hours   Cooking time: 15 minutes

Ingredients

Cottage cheese *(paneer)* (p. 8) *1 kg*
Capsicum (Shimla *mirch) 20 gm / 4 tsp*
Tomatoes *20 gm / 4 tsp*
Onions *20 gm / 4 tsp*
Pineapple *(ananas) 20 gm / 4 tsp*
Caraway seeds *(shahi jeera)*
3 gm / ½ tsp
White pepper *(safed mirch)* powder
5 gm / 1 tsp
Garam masala (p. 6) *10 gm / 2 tsp*
Turmeric *(haldi)* powder *5 gm / 1 tsp*
Lemon juice *15 ml / 1 tbsp*
Salt to taste
Cream *100 ml / ½ cup*
Yoghurt *(dahi)* (p. 6), drained
150 gm / ¾ cup
Gram flour *(besan)* / cornflour
(makkai ka atta) 30 gm / 2 tbsp

Red chilli powder *10 gm / 2 tsp*
Saffron *(kesar) 3 gm / ½ tsp*
Ginger *(adrak)* paste (p. 8) *15 gm / 1 tbsp*
Garlic *(lasan)* paste (p. 8) *15 gm / 1 tbsp*
Butter for basting
Chaat masala (optional) *10 gm / 2 tsp*

Method

1. Wash and cut the cottage cheese, vegetables and pineapple into 4-cm cubes.
2. Mix caraway seeds, white pepper, garam masala, turmeric powder, two-thirds of the lemon juice and salt together. Add the cottage cheese cubes to this mixture and refrigerate for 1 hour.
3. Mix together cream, yoghurt and gram flour/cornflour. Add remaining ingredients (except butter and chaat masala) and whisk to a fine batter.

16

4. Add the refrigerated cottage cheese cubes, pineapple cubes and vegetables to the batter and leave to marinate for at least 1 hour.

5. Preheat oven to 150-175 °C / 300-350 °F.

6. Skewer 6 cottage cheese cubes and 4 vegetable-pineapple pieces per skewer (one portion) and pack tightly together.

7. Roast in an oven/tandoor/charcoal grill for 5-6 minutes, basting regularly with melted butter.

8. Sprinkle chaat masala and the remaining lemon juice. Serve hot, garnished with slices of cucumber, tomato and onion.

———— ❖ ————

Drip(less) Tomatoes

While making a mixed vegetable salad,
cut the tomatoes in vertical slices;
they will drip less.

———— ❖ ————

ASSORTED FRITTERS

Serves: 6   Preparation time: 10 minutes   Cooking time: 30 minutes

Ingredients

Gram flour *(besan)*, sifted
135 gm / ³/₄ cup
Clarified butter *(ghee)* / oil *10 ml / 2 tsp*
Lemon juice *15 ml / 1 tbsp*
Cayenne pepper *(*Kashmiri *lal mirch)*
a pinch
Turmeric *(haldi)* powder *a pinch*
Garam masala (p. 6) *5 gm / 1 tsp*
Coriander *(dhaniya)* powder
10 gm / 2 tsp
Salt *5 gm / 1 tsp*
Water, cold *135 ml / ³/₄ cup*
Baking powder (optional) *3 gm / ¹/₂ tsp*
Oil for frying
Fritter options:
Potatoes—cut into rounds
Cauliflower *(phool gobi)* florets
Spinach *(palak)*, medium-sized leaves
Green chillies, medium, slit lengthwise
and filled with chaat masala
Cottage cheese *(paneer)* (p. 8), cut into 2" x 4" slices
with chaat masala layered between 2 slices

Method

1. Mix the gram flour, clarified butter, lemon juice, cayenne pepper, turmeric powder, garam masala, coriander and salt well. Add 5 tbsp water. Whisk well to make the batter lump-free. Slowly mix in more water till the consistency of batter resembles heavy cream and coats easily on the spoon.

2. Whisk for 3-5 minutes to lighten the batter more. Stir in baking powder if a cake-like crust is preferred.

3. Heat oil in a wok *(kadhai)* till it starts smoking.

4. Dip fritters in the batter and slip one by one into the hot oil. Do not allow them to stick to each other. Deep fry till crisp and golden brown. Serve hot.

COTTAGE CHEESE SEEKH KEBABS

Serves: 4-5   Preparation time: 15 minutes   Cooking time: 15 minutes

Ingredients

Cottage cheese (*paneer*) (p. 8),
finely grated *1 kg*
Garam masala (p. 6) *10 gm / 2 tsp*
Ginger (*adrak*) paste (p. 8)
25 gm / 5 tsp
Green chillies, chopped *6*
Lemon juice *15 ml / 1 tbsp*
Onions, grated *150 gm / ¾ cup*
Red chilli powder *5 gm / 1 tsp*
Salt for seasoning
White pepper (*safed mirch*) powder
5 gm / 1 tsp
Butter for basting *20 gm / 4 tsp*
Cornflour (*makkai ka atta*)
15 gm / 1 tbsp

Method

1. Mix all the ingredients, adding the cornflour in the end.
2. Divide this mixture into 15 equal balls.
3. Preheat the oven to 150-175 °C / 300-350 °F.
4. Skewer each ball. Spread by pressing along the length of the skewer with a wet hand, making each kebab about 8-10 cm long, 1 cm apart.
5. Roast in oven/tandoor/charcoal grill for 5-6 minutes. Baste with melted butter and roast for another 2 minutes. Remove from skewers.
6. Garnish with slices of cucumber, tomato, onion and serve hot, accompanied by chutney (p. 86).

STIR-FRIED MUSHROOMS

Serves: 4   Preparation time: 10 minutes   Cooking time: 20 minutes

Ingredients

Mushrooms (*guchi*) ½ kg
Oil *22 ml / 4 ½ tsp*
Onions, sliced *2*
Garlic (*lasan*) paste (p. 8) *5 gm / 1 tsp*
Tomato, chopped *1*
Turmeric *(haldi)* powder *3 gm / ½ tsp*
Garam masala (p. 6) *3 gm / ½ tsp*
Red chilli powder *3 gm / ½ tsp*
Salt to taste
Green coriander (*hara dhaniya*),
chopped *15 gm / 1 tbsp*

Method

1. Cut mushrooms into slices.
2. Heat oil and fry onions until golden in colour. Add garlic paste and chopped tomato; mix well.
3. Put in turmeric powder, garam masala, chilli powder and salt and fry for 3-4 minutes. Stir in mushrooms and simmer until the mushrooms are tender, adding very little water if necessary.
4. Garnish with coriander and serve hot.

BEANS PORIYAL

(Beans with split black gram)

Serves: 4-5   Preparation time: 25 minutes   Cooking time: 20 minutes

Ingredients

Beans (*sem*) *1 kg*
Turmeric (*haldi*) powder *2 gm / ½ tsp*
Salt *5 gm / 1 tsp*
Oil *60 ml / 4 tbsp*
Mustard (*rai*) seeds *5 gm / 1 tsp*
Black gram, split (*dhuli urad dal*)
5 gm / 1 tsp
Red chillies, whole *2*
Onions, chopped *2*
Green chillies, chopped *2*
Salt to taste
Coconut (*nariyal*), fresh, grated *½*

Method

1. Remove the strings from the beans and chop finely.
2. Boil the beans in 1 cup of water, adding turmeric powder and salt. Cook until the beans are almost done. Drain excess water and keep aside.
3. Heat oil in a wok (*kadhai*). Add mustard seeds, split black gram and whole red chillies. When mustard seeds begin to crackle, add chopped onions and green chillies.
4. Stir-fry for 4-5 minutes.
5. Add beans and stir-fry till beans are cooked.
6. Add salt to taste and the grated coconut; stir and remove from fire.
7. Serve immediately, accompanied by a curry dish and steamed rice or *paranthas*.

CRUNCHY OKRA

Serves: 4-6   Preparation time: 40 minutes   Cooking time: 30 minutes

Ingredients

Okra *(bhindi)* ½ kg
Salt to taste
Red chilli powder *5 gm / 1 tsp*
Garam masala (p. 6) *5 gm / 1 tsp*
Raw mango powder *(amchoor)*
3 gm / ½ tsp
Chaat masala *3 gm / ½ tsp*
Gram flour *(besan) 45 gm / 3 tbsp*
Oil for frying
Ginger *(adrak)*, julienned (long, thin
strips) *7 gm / 1 ½ tsp*
Green chillies, sliced (optional) *2*
Carom *(ajwain)* seeds *3 gm / ½ tsp*

Method

1. Snip off both ends of each okra and slice lengthwise into four slices.
2. Spread the slices on a flat dish; sprinkle evenly with salt, red chilli powder, garam masala, mango powder and chaat masala. Mix gently to coat okra evenly.
3. Sprinkle gram flour over the okra slices and mix to coat evenly, preferably without adding any water.
4. Divide the okra into two portions. Heat oil in a wok *(kadhai)* or a pan till it starts smoking. Fry one portion of coated okra slices, separating each lightly with a fork. Do not allow the slices to stick to each other.
5. Remove when both sides are crisp and brown in colour. Fry the other portion in the same way.
6. Garnish with julienned ginger and green chillies and serve at once.

BHARWAN KARELAS

(Stuffed bitter gourds)

Serves: 4   Preparation time: 1 hour   Cooking time: 45 minutes

Ingredients

Bitter gourds (*karela*) *1 kg*
Mustard oil (*sarson ka tel*) for frying
Clarified butter (*ghee*) *60 gm / ¼ cup*
Asafoetida (*hing*) powder *a pinch*
Yoghurt (*dahi*) (p. 6) *100 gm / ½ cup*
Salt to taste
Red chilli powder *5 gm / 1 tsp*
Ginger (*adrak*) paste (p. 8) *5 gm / 1 tsp*
Onion paste (p. 8) *60 gm / ¼ cup*
Garlic (*lasan*) paste (p. 8) *10 gm / 2 tsp*
Ginger (*adrak*), chopped
10 gm / 2 tsp
Green chillies, chopped *10 gm / 2 tsp*
Green coriander (*hara dhaniya*),
chopped *5 gm / 1 tsp*
Water *100 ml / ½ cup*

For the filling:

Sugar *10 gm / 2 tsp*
Salt *10 gm / 2 tsp*
Potatoes, boiled, cut into
½" cubes *120 gm / ½ cup*
Cumin (*jeera*) *3 gm / ½ tsp*
Bengal gram (*chana dal*), boiled,
drained *120 gm / ½ cup*
Tamarind (*imli*) pulp *10 gm / 2 tsp*
Fennel (*saunf*) *10 gm / 2 tsp*
Red chilli powder *5 gm / 1 tsp*
Mustard oil *(sarson ka tel)* *45 ml / 3 tbsp*

Method

1. Scrape the bitter gourds and boil them in water till half cooked. Slit, remove seeds and squeeze them gently to remove water.

2. Heat mustard oil in a wok *(kadhai)*; deep fry the bitter gourds till crisp. Keep aside.

3. Heat clarified butter in a pan. Add asafoetida along with all the other ingredients. Stir-fry for a few minutes, add water and cook till the water evaporates. Remove from heat.

4. Stuff the bitter gourds with the filling mixture (leave aside the mustard oil) and tie with a thread.

5. In a separate pan, heat 45 ml mustard oil; add all the other ingredients along with the bitter gourds and cook till moisture evaporates. Remove and serve hot.

Nourishing Nutrients

To avoid any wastage of vitamins and minerals, pare or scrape the vegetables as thinly as possible for the nutrients lie very close to the skin.

ALU KI TARKARI

(Spiced potato creoles)

Serves: 4-5   Preparation time: 10 minutes   Cooking time: 30 minutes

Ingredients

Potatoes, boiled, cubed
900 gm / 4 ½ cups
Oil *80 ml / 5 ⅓ tbsp*
Red chillies, cut into half *5*
Mustard *(rai)* seeds *5 gm / 1 tsp*
Onions, chopped *100 gm / ½ cup*
Garlic *(lasan)*, chopped *20 gm / 4 tsp*
Ginger *(adrak)*, chopped *20 gm / 4 tsp*
Red chilli powder *10 gm / 2 tsp*
Turmeric *(haldi)* powder *5 gm / 1 tsp*
Coriander *(dhaniya)* powder
8 gm / 1 ⅔ tsp
Salt for seasoning
Tomatoes, skinned, chopped
300 gm / 1 ½ cups
Green chillies, chopped *10 gm / 2 tsp*

Lemon juice *15 ml / 1 tbsp*
Butter *(makhan) 20 gm / 4 tsp*

Method

1. Heat the oil in a pan and sauté the red chillies and mustard seeds over medium heat.
2. Add the chopped onions, garlic and ginger; sauté over high heat for 5-6 minutes. Add the red chilli, turmeric and coriander powders; add salt and stir.
3. Add the chopped tomatoes and simmer on low heat until the oil separates from the gravy.
4. Add the boiled potato cubes, green chillies, lemon juice and salt; stir and cook for 5 minutes.
5. Melt the butter and pour over the potatoes before serving. Garnish with green coriander.

BHARWAN SHIMLA MIRCH

(Stuffed capsicums)

Serves: 4   Preparation time: 30 minutes   Cooking time: 45 minutes

Ingredients

Capsicums (Shimla *mirch*) *600 gm*
Oil *60 ml / 3 ½ tbsp*
Ginger (*adrak*), chopped *15 gm / 1 tbsp*
Cumin (*jeera*) seeds *10 gm / 2 tsp*
Potatoes, boiled, diced *100 gm / ½ cup*
Cottage cheese *(paneer)* (p. 8),
cubed *100 gm / ½ cup*
Red chilli powder *15 gm / 1 tbsp*
Turmeric (*haldi*) powder *10 gm / 2 tsp*
Garam masala (p. 6) *5 gm / 1 tsp*
Cumin (*jeera*) powder *15 gm / 1 tbsp*
Cashewnuts (*kaju*) *45 gm / 3 tbsp*
Raisins (*kishmish*) *25 gm / 5 tsp*
Green chillies, chopped *15 gm / 1 tbsp*
Green coriander *(hara dhaniya)*,
chopped *15 gm / 1 tbsp*

Salt to taste
For the marinade:
Yoghurt (*dahi*) (p. 6), hung *200 gm / 1 cup*
Red chilli paste (p. 6) *20 gm / 4 tsp*
Ginger-garlic (*adrak-lasan*) paste
(p. 8) *20 gm / 4 tsp*
Garam masala (p. 6) *3 gm / ½ tsp*
Salt to taste
Butter for basting
Cumin (*jeera*) powder *3 gm / ½ tsp*

Method

1. Remove tops of capsicums and keep aside. Scoop out the seeds from the capsicum cups.
2. Heat oil in a wok *(kadhai)*. Add ginger and cumin seeds; sauté till they crackle. Add potatoes and

cottage cheese. Sauté for a few minutes. Stir in dry spices along with the remaining ingredients. Mix well and remove from wok.

3. Fill the capsicums with this mixture and cover with the tops.

4. For the marinade, mix all the ingredients and coat the capsicums with it.

5. Skewer the capsicums and cook in a tandoor/oven/grill for 10 minutes. Remove, baste with butter and cook further for 2-5 minutes. Serve hot.

———— ❖ ————

Steam(y) Matters

Vegetables that tend to give off a lot of water while cooking should be cooked uncovered to let the steam escape fast.

———— ❖ ————

ANJEERI KUM-KUM

(Delicious mushrooms stuffed with figs)

Serves: 4-5   Preparation time: 45 minutes   Cooking time: 5 minutes

Ingredients

Figs *(anjeer)*, dried *300 gm / 1½ cups*
Garam masala (p. 6) *4 gm / ¾ tsp*
Garlic *(lasan)*, grated *3 gm / ²/₃ tsp*
Ginger *(adrak)*, grated *3 gm / ²/₃ tsp*
Green chillies *5 gm / 1 tsp*
Lemon juice *5 ml / 1 tsp*
Onion, grated *10 gm / 2 tsp*
White pepper *(safed mirch)* powder
2 gm / ½ tsp
Mushrooms *(guchi) 600 gm / 3 cups*
Refined oil *10 ml / 2 tsp*
Saffron *(kesar) 2 gm*
Milk (to dissolve saffron) *10 ml / 2 tsp*
Salt to taste

Method

1. Soak the dried figs in lukewarm water for 20 minutes. Drain, wipe and chop very fine. Add all the other ingredients except the mushrooms, oil, milk and saffron. Season to taste.

2. Stuff each mushroom with 8-10 gm of the mixture and keep aside for 20 minutes.

3. Heat the oil in a pan till moderately hot. Arrange the mushrooms in the pan and let them cook on low heat for a minute. Turn the mushrooms over and cook for another minute. Or place the mushrooms on a greased baking dish and bake in a moderately hot oven for 5 minutes.

4. Remove the mushrooms from pan/oven; brush with saffron dissolved in milk and serve immediately.

PANEER TAWA MASALA

(Stir-fried cottage cheese cooked on a griddle)

Serves: 4   Preparation time: 20 minutes   Cooking time: 30 minutes

Ingredients

Cottage cheese (*paneer*) (p. 8),
cubed *700 gm / 3 ½ cups*
Clarified butter (*ghee*)
100 gm / ½ cup
Carom (*ajwain*) seeds *5 gm / 1 tsp*
Onions, chopped *200 gm / 1 cup*
Ginger (*adrak*), chopped *15 gm / 3 tsp*
Green chillies, chopped *5*
Red chilli powder *5 gm / 1 tsp*
Coriander (*dhaniya*) powder
5 gm / 1 tsp
Salt to taste
Garam masala (p. 6) *5 gm / 1 tsp*
Green coriander (*hara dhaniya*),
chopped *10 gm / 2 tsp*
For the *makhni* gravy:

Tomatoes *1 kg*
Ginger-garlic (*adrak-lasan*) paste (p. 8) *30 gm / 2 tbsp*
Green chillies *10*
Cloves (*laung*) powder *5 gm / 1 tsp*
Green cardamom (*choti elaichi*) powder *5 gm / 1 tsp*
Water *500 ml / 2 ½ cups*
Salt to taste
Butter *200 gm / 1 cup*
Cream *150 gm / ¾ cup*
Dry fenugreek (*kasoori methi*) powder *10 gm / 2 tsp*
Garam masala (p. 6) *5 gm / 1 tsp*

Method

1. Heat clarified butter in a griddle (*tawa*). Add carom seeds and sauté till they crackle. Add onions, ginger, green chillies and sauté for 5 minutes.
2. Stir in red chilli powder, coriander powder and salt

along with cottage cheese cubes and stir for a minute.

3. Stir in the *makhni* gravy (see below), cover and cook till it thickens and the cottage cheese cubes are coated with it.

For the *makhni* gravy, heat a pot (*handi*); add all the ingredients except butter, cream, dry feungreek powder and garam masala. Cook for 30 minutes, mashing continuously.

4. Strain and return to heat. Cook till the gravy thickens; add the remaining ingredients. Cook for 5 minutes more.

5. Remove from heat. Garnish with garam masala and green coriander and serve hot.

------------ ❖ ------------

Softer Options

Dip cottage cheese in salt water before adding to a curry or gravy. This will make it soft.

------------ ❖ ------------

METHI CHAMAN

(Cottage cheese cubes in an exotic fenugreek and spinach purée)

Serves: 4-5   Preparation time: 10 minutes   Cooking time: 1 hour

Ingredients

Fresh fenugreek *(methi) 150 gm*
Cottage cheese *(paneer)* (p. 8), small
cubes *500 gm / 2 ½ cups*
Spinach *(palak) 450 gm / 2 ¼ cups*
Oil *30 ml / 2 tbsp,* Salt to taste
Butter *(makhan) 30 gm / 2 tbsp*
Onions, grated *50 gm / 3 ⅓ tbsp*
Ginger *(adrak)* paste (p. 8)
50 gm / ¼ cup
Green chilli paste (p. 6) *15 gm / 3 tsp*
Garlic *(lasan)*, chopped *10 gm / 2 tsp*
White pepper *(safed mirch)* powder *5
gm / 1 tsp*
Red chilli powder *5 gm / 1 tsp*
Garam masala (p. 6) *8 gm / 1 ⅔ tsp*
Ginger *(adrak)*, chopped *5 gm / 1 tsp*

Method

1. Wash fenugreek and spinach and chop the leaves. Blanch in salt water for 1 minute. Remove, cool and blend in a food processor to a fine purée.
2. Heat the oil and butter in a wok *(kadhai)*. Add the onions, ginger, green chilli paste and chopped garlic. Sauté over low heat for 5-6 minutes. Add pepper, salt and red chillies.
3. Add the fenugreek and spinach purée and cook for 35-40 minutes until the oil separates.
4. Add the cottage cheese cubes and sprinkle garam masala. Cover and cook for 10 minutes.
5. Garnish with ginger and serve with any Indian bread of choice (pp. 88-91).

CRISPY CAULIFLOWER

Serves: 4-5   Preparation time: 15 minutes   Cooking time: 15 minutes

Ingredients

Cauliflowers (*phool gobi*), small 5
whole ones *1 kg*
Salt to taste
Turmeric *(haldi)* powder *10 gm / 2
tsp*
Gram flour *(besan)* / flour *(maida)* /
maize flour *(makkai ka atta)*
200 gm / 1 cup
Carom *(ajwain)* seeds *6 gm / 1 tsp*
Lemon juice *3 ml / ²/₃ tsp*
Yoghurt *(dahi)* (p. 6) *100 gm / ½ cup*
Ginger *(adrak)* paste (p. 8)
10 gm / 2 tsp
Garlic *(lasan)* paste (p. 8)
10 gm / 2 tsp
Garam masala (p. 6) *8 gm / 1 ²/₃ tsp*
Red / yellow chilli powder
10 gm / 2 tsp

Oil *500 ml / 2 ½ cups*
Green coriander (*hara dhaniya*),
finely chopped *20 gm / 4 tsp*
Green chillies, finely chopped
20 gm / 4 tsp

Method

1. Boil sufficient water to immerse the cauliflowers. Add salt and turmeric powder.
2. Gradually add the cauliflowers to this brine solution. Cook for 8-10 minutes over medium heat until the cauliflowers are half cooked. Drain and keep aside
3. In a bowl, make a batter with the gram flour/white flour/maize flour, carom seeds, lemon juice, yoghurt, ginger and garlic pastes, garam masala, chilli powder and salt. The batter should be thick and smooth.
4. Heat the oil in a wok (*kadhai*). Dip each cauliflower

into the batter, coat evenly and deep fry over medium heat till golden brown.

5. Cut each cauliflower into four parts and place on a platter, garnished with green coriander and green chillies. Serve with fresh cucumbers and sliced tomatoes.

——— ❖ ———

White on White!

To preserve the white colour of cauliflower, add a teaspoon of milk or milk powder while cooking it.

——— ❖ ———

ALU-PALAK

(Ginger-flavoured potatoes in spinach cream)

Serves: 4-5 Preparation time: 25 minutes Cooking time: 25 minutes

Ingredients

Potatoes, boiled *250 gm / 1 ¼ cups*
Spinach *(palak) 1 kg*
Water *2 lt / 10 cups*
Salt to taste
Maize flour *(makkai ka atta)*
10 gm / 2 tsp
Clarified butter *(ghee) 30 gm / 2 tbsp*
Onions, chopped *25 gm / 5 tsp*
Ginger *(adrak)*, chopped fine
25 gm / 5 tsp
Red chilli powder *5 gm / 1 tsp* or
green chillies, chopped *3*
Cream *10 gm / 2 tsp*

Method

1. Remove the stalks of the spinach leaves. Wash and chop fine. Add water and salt and cook for about 10 minutes. Drain the water and purée the spinach.
2. Add the potato cubes to the purée and mix well.
3. Gradually stir in the maize flour and cook for 10 minutes. (This acts as a thickening agent.)
4. In a separate pan, heat the clarified butter and brown the onions and half the ginger. Add the red chilli powder / green chillies and sauté for a minute.
5. Pour this over the potato-spinach mixture, stir well and heat through. Serve, garnished with ginger juliennes and cream, accompanied by a *dal,* green salad and any Indian bread of choice (pp. 88-91).

BAGHAR-E-BAIGAN

(Aubergines tempered with fenugreek and garlic)

Serves: 4-5   Preparation time: 10 minutes   Cooking time: 20 minutes

Ingredients

Aubergines *(baigan)*, medium
500 gm / ½ kg
Tamarind *(imli) 50 gm / 3 ¹/₃ tbsp*
Onions, chopped *200 gm / 1 cup*
Ginger *(adrak)* paste (p. 8)
30 gm / 2 tbsp
Garlic *(lasan)* paste (p. 8)
30 gm / 2 tbsp
Sesame seeds *(til) 15 gm / 3 tsp*
Coconut *(nariyal)*, desiccated
15 gm / 3 tsp
Red chilli powder *15 gm / 3 tsp*
Coriander *(dhaniya)* powder
15 gm / 3 tsp
Oil *200 ml / 1 cup*
Curry leaves *(meethi neem ke patte) 3*

Cumin *(jeera)* powder *10 gm / 2 tsp*
Fenugreek seeds *(methi dana) 1 gm / ¼ tsp*
Garlic *(lasan)* cloves, chopped *30 gm / 2 tbsp*
Turmeric *(haldi)* powder *5 gm / 1 tsp*
Salt to taste

Method

1. Soak the tamarind in warm water and squeeze out the pulp.
2. Quarter all the aubergines without disjoining them from the stem.
3. Grind the onions and ginger and garlic pastes to a fine mixture.
4. Roast the sesame seeds, coconut, chilli powder and coriander powder. Add 15 ml water and grind to a fine paste.

5. Heat the oil in a pan; add the curry leaves, cumin, fenugreek and garlic cloves and sauté for the *baghar* (tempering).

6. Add the ground spices, aubergines, tamarind pulp, turmeric powder, salt and ½ cup of water to the *baghar* and cook on a low fire till the aubergines become tender. Serve with steamed rice.

—————— ❖ ——————

The Goodness of Garlic

To remove the skin from garlic cloves easily, slice the cloves half down the convex side. The peels will come off easily. If you chop garlic with a little salt, it will not stick to the knife or the chopping board.

—————— ❖ ——————

ALU GOBI SUKHI

(Peppy potatoes and spicy cauliflower)

Serves: 4-5 Preparation time: 10 minutes Cooking time: 40 minutes

Ingredients

Potatoes, medium, cut into quarters
500 gm / 2 ½ cups
Cauliflower *(phool gobhi)*, cut into
small pieces *500 gm / 2 ½ cups*
Oil *80 ml / ⅓ cup*
Bayleaves *(tej patta) 2*
Green cardamoms *(choti elaichi) 5*
Red chillies, whole, cut into half *5*
Cumin *(jeera)* seeds *6 gm / 1 ⅓ tsp*
Onions, chopped *100 gm / ½ cup*
Ginger *(adrak)* paste (p. 8)
40 gm / 2 ⅔ tbsp
Garlic *(lasan)* paste (p. 8)
40 gm / 2 ⅔ tbsp
Turmeric *(haldi)* powder *5 gm / 1 tsp*
Red chilli powder *8 gm / 1 ⅔ tsp*

Coriander *(dhaniya)* powder *10 gm / 2 tsp*
Tomatoes, chopped *200 gm / 1 cup*
Salt for seasoning
Black pepper *(kali mirch)*, crushed *5*
Garam masala (p. 6) *15 gm / 3 tsp*
Green coriander *(hara dhaniya)*, chopped *15 gm / 1 tbsp*
Ginger *(adrak)*, julienned *(*long, thin strips) *10 gm / 2 tsp*

Method

1. Heat the oil in a pan. Add the bayleaves, cardamoms, whole red chillies and cumin seeds. Sauté over medium heat.

2. Add the chopped onions, ginger-garlic paste, turmeric powder, red chilli powder and coriander powder; sauté for 45-60 seconds. Add tomatoes and cook for another 5 minutes.

3. Add the cauliflower and potatoes and cook over medium heat for 10 minutes. Add 200 ml / 1 cup of water, cover and cook for 10 minutes on low heat. Season with salt, black pepper and garam masala and stir.

4. Serve, garnished with green coriander and ginger juliennes, as an accompaniment to any Indian bread of choice (pp. 88-91).

———— ❖ ————

Dress Up Your Table

Take small, tender cucumbers, slit them lengthwise and remove the seeds. Put the cucumbers in a plastic bag and chill them. Just before serving, fill up the hollow spaces with chopped raw vegetables. You can now serve cucumber boats on the table.

———— ❖ ————

PALAK PANEER

(Spinach and cottage cheese curry)

Serves: 4-5   Preparation time: 25 minutes   Cooking time: 30 minutes

Ingredients

Spinach *(palak)* leaves 1 kg
Cottage cheese *(paneer)* (p. 8),
cubed *250 gm / 1¼ cups*
Water *2 lt / 10 cups*
Salt to taste
Maize flour *(makkai ka atta)*
20 gm / 4 tsp
Clarified butter *(ghee) 30 gm / 2 tbsp*
Onions, chopped *25 gm / 5 tsp*
Ginger *(adrak)*, finely cut *25 gm / 5 tsp*
Red chilli powder *5 gm / 1 tsp*
Tomato, finely cut *10 gm / 2 tsp*
Green chillies, chopped *3*
Cream *10 gm / 2 tsp*

Method

1. Remove the stalks of the spinach leaves. Wash and cut finely. Add water and salt; cook for 10 minutes. Drain the excess water and purée in a blender.
2. Add the cottage cheese cubes to the purée and mix well. Slowly stir in the maize flour and cook for 10 minutes. (This acts as a thickening agent.)
3. In a separate pan, heat the clarified butter. Brown the onions and most of the ginger. Add red chilli powder and stir. Pour this sauce over the spinach-cottage cheese mixture. Stir well and cook for 5 minutes.
4. Garnish with the remaining ginger, tomato pieces, green chillies and cream. Serve with a green salad and any bread of choice (pp. 88-91).

COTTAGE CHEESE COOKED IN A WOK

Serves: 4   Preparation time: 15 minutes   Cooking time: 10 minutes

Ingredients

Cottage cheese *(paneer)* (p. 8) *600 gm*
Capsicum (Shimla *mirch*)
45 gm / 3 tbsp
Red chillies, whole *15*
Coriander *(dhaniya)* seeds
10 gm / 2 tsp
Oil *45 ml / 3 tbsp*
Onions, chopped *45 gm / 3 tbsp*
Ginger *(adrak)*, julienned (long, thin
strips) *15 gm / 1 tbsp*
Tomato purée (p. 8) *150 ml / ¾ cup*
Salt to taste
Fenugreek *(methi)* powder *5 gm / 1 tsp*
Garam masala (p. 6) *8 gm / 1½ tsp*
Coriander powder *10 gm / 2 tsp*
Black pepper *(kali mirch) 8 gm / 1½ tsp*
Green coriander *(hara dhaniya)*,
chopped *15 gm / 1 tbsp*

Method

1. Cut the cottage cheese into fingers. Cut the capsicum into half, deseed and make juliennes.
2. Powder red chillies and coriander seeds in a pestle.
3. Heat the oil in a wok *(kadhai)*, sauté the onions and capsicum over medium heat for 2 minutes.
4. Add the pounded spices and two-thirds of the ginger and stir for 1 minute.
5. Add the tomato purée and salt. Bring to a boil. Simmer until the oil separates from the gravy.
6. Add the cottage cheese and stir gently for 2-3 minutes.
7. Stir in fenugreek powder, garam masala, coriander powder and black pepper.
8. Garnish with chopped coriander and the remaining julienned ginger. Serve hot.

CREAMY BLACK GRAM

Serves: 4   Preparation time: 20 minutes   Cooking time: 1 hour

Ingredients

Black gram (*urad dal*)
120 gm / 1 cup
Water *1½ lt / 7½ cups*
Salt to taste
Ginger-garlic (*adrak-lasan*) paste
(p. 8) *45 gm / 3 tbsp*
Tomato purée (p. 8) *120 ml / ½ cup*
Red chilli paste (p. 6) *25 gm / 5 tsp*
White butter *(safed makhan)*
120 gm / ½ cup
Cream *120 gm / ½ cup*
Green coriander (*hara dhaniya*),
chopped *10 gm / 2 tsp*

Method

1. Soak black gram in water and boil along with salt until the black gram is tender and the water has reduced to one-fourth.

2. Stir in ginger-garlic paste, tomato purée, red chilli paste, white butter and cream. Mix well and cook for about 45 minutes on very low heat.

3. Adjust seasoning to taste and cook further for 5 minutes.

4. Remove from heat into a serving bowl. Sprinkle cream on top and garnish with chopped green coriander. Serve hot.

DUM ALOO KASHMIRI

(Kashmiri-style, slow-cooked potatoes)

Serves: 4   Preparation time: 2 hours 30 minutes   Cooking time: 25 minutes

Ingredients

Potatoes (medium) *8*
Oil *100 ml / ½ cup*
Caraway seeds *(shahi jeera)*
5 gm / 1 tsp
Aniseed *(saunf) 5 gm / 1 tsp*
Onions, chopped *2*
Black cardamom *(bari elaichi)*,
pounded *5 gm / 1 tsp*
Raisins *(kishmish) 75 gm / 5 tbsp*
Cashewnuts *(kaju) 75 gm / 5 tbsp*
Sate to taste
For the curry:
Onions, chopped *60 gm / 4 tbsp*
Yoghurt *(dahi)* (p. 6), whisked
225 gm / 1¼ cups
Tomato purée (p. 8) *200 ml / 1 cup*

Ginger-garlic *(adrak-lasan)* paste (p. 8) *20 gm / 4 tsp*
Almond *(badam)* paste *40 gm / 2 ¾ tbsp*
Aniseed *(saunf) 5 gm / 1tsp*
Mace *(javitri)* powder *3 gm / ½ tsp*
Caraway seeds (shahi jeera) *2 gm / ½ tsp*
Green cardamoms *(choti elaichi) 4*
Cloves *(laung) 6*
Red chilli paste (p. 8) *20 gm / 4 tsp*
Cumin *(jeera)* powder *10 gm / 2 tsp*
Coriander *(dhaniya)* powder *15 gm / 1 tbsp*
Salt to taste
Oil for frying

Method

1. Peel potatoes, slice off the tops. Scoop out the centres. Fry the shells and centres to golden brown. Allow the centres to cool and mash.

2. Heat oil in a wok *(kadhai);* sauté caraway seeds and aniseed. Add onions and sauté till transparent. Add the fried potato centres, cardamom powder, raisins and cashewnuts. Stir-fry for a few minutes. Season with salt. Keep aside.

3. Stuff the fried shells with the prepared mixture and keep aside.

4. For the curry, heat oil in a thick-bottomed pan. Sauté onions till transparent. Add yoghurt, tomato purée, ginger-garlic pastes, almond paste, aniseed, mace, caraway seeds, green cardamoms, cloves, red chilli paste, cumin powder, coriander powder and salt. Stir-fry for 8-10 minutes.

5. Place the stuffed potatoes in the curry; cover the lid and seal with dough. Cook on slow fire for 10 minutes. Remove from heat. Place the potatoes in a serving dish, strain the curry and pour on top of the potatoes.

6. Serve immediately, accompanied by any Indian bread of choice (pp. 88-91).

❖

Piping Hot Rotis

If you want to serve rotis to your guests and have no help, don't worry. Half-cook and wrap in a clean napkin. After laying the table, bake them again on the griddle.

❖

MUSHROOM, CAPSICUM AND CABBAGE CURRY

Serves: 4-5   Preparation time: 10 minutes   Cooking time: 15 minutes

Ingredients

Mushrooms (*guchi*), quartered
600 gm / 3 cups
Cabbage (*band gobi*), shredded
120 gm / ½ cup
Capsicums (Shimla *mirch*), julienned
(long thin strips) *60 gm / 4 tbsp*
Red chillies, whole *4*
Coriander (*dhaniya*) seeds *5 gm / 1 tsp*
Oil *120 gm / ½ cup*
Onions, sliced *80 gm / ⅓ cup*
Garlic (*lasan*) paste (p. 8) *20 gm / 4 tsp*
Salt to taste
Garam masala (p. 6) *10 gm / 2 tsp*
Tomatoes, chopped *500 gm / 2½ cups*
Green chillies, chopped *4*
Ginger (*adrak*), chopped *30 gm / 2 tbsp*
Green coriander (*hara dhaniya*),
chopped *20 gm / 4 tsp*

Method

1. Pound red chillies and coriander seeds with a pestle.
2. Heat 2 tbsp oil in a wok. Stir-fry mushrooms over medium heat for a few minutes. Remove and keep.
3. In the same oil, stir-fry the cabbage until the liquid evaporates.
4. Heat the remaining oil in a wok (*kadhai*). Sauté the onions till transparent. Add the garlic paste and stir for 20 seconds over medium heat.
5. Add the red chillies, coriander seeds, garam masala and salt. Stir for 30 seconds. Add tomatoes and cook till the oil separates from the mixture.
6. Stir in green chillies, ginger and half the green coriander. Add stir-fried mushrooms and cabbage; cook for a few minutes. Garnish with julienned capsicums and remaining green coriander. Serve hot.

SHAHI PANEER

(Cottage cheese in a rich gravy)

Serves: 4-5   Preparation time: 30 minutes   Cooking time: 20 minutes

Ingredients

Cottage cheese (*paneer*) (p. 8),
fingers *1 kg*
Oil *80 ml / 5 ¹/₃ tbsp*
Cloves (*laung*) *6*
Bayleaves *(tej patta) 2*
Cinnamon (*dalchini*) sticks *3*
Green cardamoms (*choti elaichi*) *6*
Onion paste (p. 8) *200 gm / 1 cup*
Ginger (*adrak*) paste (p. 8)
40 gm / 2 ²/₃ tbsp
Garlic (*lasan*) paste (p. 8)
40 gm / 2 ²/₃ tbsp
Red chilli powder *10 gm / 2 tsp*
Turmeric (*haldi*) powder *4 gm / ³/₄ tsp*
Coriander (*dhaniya*) powder
5 gm / 1 tsp

Cashewnut *(kaju)* paste *10 gm / 2 tsp*
Salt to taste
Red colouring *¹/₃ tsp*
Yoghurt (*dahi*) (p. 6), whisked *180 gm / ³/₄ cup*
Sugar *10 gm / 2 tsp*
Cream *120 ml / ²/₃ cup*
Garam masala (p. 6) *8 gm / 1 ²/₃ tsp*
Green cardamom *(choti elaichi)* powder *3 gm / ²/₃ tsp*
Mace *(javitri)* powder *3 gm / ²/₃ tsp*
Vetivier *(kewda) 3 drops*
Saffron *(kesar)*, dissolved in 1 tbsp milk *½ gm*

Method

1. Heat the oil in a pan. Add cloves, bayleaves, cinnamon sticks and green cardamoms. Sauté over medium heat until they begin to crackle. Add the onion paste and stir-fry for 2-3 minutes.

2. Stir in the ginger and garlic pastes, red chilli powder, turmeric powder, coriander powder, cashewnut paste, salt and colouring.

3. Add yoghurt, ½ cup warm water and sugar; bring to a slow boil and then simmer until the oil separates.

4. Allow the curry to cool. Remove whole spices and blend to a smooth consistency.

5. Reheat the curry, stir in the cream, garam masala, cardamom powder, mace powder, vetivier and saffron mixture.

6. Add the cottage cheese fingers and cook for another 5 minutes.

7. Serve hot, garnished with chopped coriander.

---- ❖ ----

Fresh Breath

*To get rid of onion-breath, eat a
few coriander seeds.*

---- ❖ ----

HYDERABADI CHILLI CURRY

Serves: 4-5   Preparation time: 15 minutes   Cooking time: 35 minutes

Ingredients

Green chillies, large, slit *200 gm / 1 cup*
Tamarind (*imli*) *60 gm / 4 tbsp*
Coconut (*nariyal*), desiccated
50 gm / ¼ cup
Peanuts (*moongphali*) *50 gm / ¼ cup*
Sesame seeds (*til*) *50 gm / 3 ⅔ tbsp*
Coriander (*dhaniya*) seeds,
roasted *20 gm / 4 tsp*
Cumin (*jeera*) powder *20 gm / 4 tsp*
Red chilli powder *12 gm / 2 ½ tsp*
Turmeric (*haldi*) powder *5 gm / 1 tsp*
Salt to taste
Brown onion paste (p. 6) *1 kg / 5 cups*
Ginger-garlic (*adrak-lasan*) paste
(p. 8) *30 gm / 2 tbsp*
Oil *500 ml / 2 ½ cups*
Mustard (*rai*) seeds *3 gm / ⅔ tsp*
Onion seeds (*kalonji*) *3 gm / ⅔ tsp*

Curry leaves (*meethi neem ke patte*) *20*
Cumin (*jeera*) seeds *3 gm / ⅔ tsp*

Method

1. Soak tamarind in warm water for 10 minutes. Squeeze out water, retain the pulp.
2. Broil the coconut, peanuts and sesame seeds. Grind to a fine paste. Mix in coriander seeds, cumin and red chilli powder, turmeric, salt, brown onion paste and ginger-garlic paste. Fill this paste into the slit and deseeded green chillies. Keep aside.
3. Heat oil in a wok (*kadhai*); fry the green chillies to golden brown. Drain excess oil and keep aside.
4. In the same oil, sauté mustard, onion and cumin seeds and curry leaves. Stir in tamarind pulp and cook on low heat for 10 minutes.
5. Add the fried green chillies, simmer for another 10 minutes and serve hot.

TOMATOES STUFFED WITH MUSHROOMS

Serves: 4-5   Preparation time: 15 minutes   Cooking time: 1 hour

Ingredients

Tomatoes (round and firm) *15*
Mushrooms (*guchi*), chopped
500 gm / 2 ½ cups
Oil *30 ml / 2 tbsp*
Onions, chopped *30 gm / 2 tbsp*
Garlic, chopped *15 gm / 1 tbsp*
Tomato pulp, fresh / canned
100 gm / ½ cup
Green chillies, finely chopped
5 gm / 1 tsp
Salt to taste
Garam masala (p. 6) *10 gm / 2 tsp*
Mint (*pudina*) leaves, chopped
10 gm / 2 tsp
Lemon juice *10 ml / 2 tsp*
Caraway seed (*shahi jeera*) powder,
roasted *2 gm / ½ tsp*
Green coriander (*hara dhaniya*),
chopped *10 gm / 2 tsp*
For the sauce:
Oil *25 ml / 5 tsp*
Green cardamom (*choti elaichi*)
powder *3 gm / ²/₃ tsp*
Bayleaf (*tej patta*) *1*
Onions, sliced *20 gm / 4 tsp*
Garlic (*lasan*) *10 gm / 2 tsp*
Tomatoes, chopped *300 gm / 1 ½ cups*
Salt to taste
Cream *60 ml / 4 tbsp*
Mace (*javitri*) powder *3 gm / ²/₃ tsp*

Method

1. Slice off the tops of the tomatoes, scoop out the pulp, drain upside down on a paper towel. Keep the tops aside.
2. Heat oil in a pan, sauté the onions, garlic and

tomato pulp over medium heat until the moisture evaporates completely and the oil separates.

3. Stir in the green chillies and mushrooms. Cook over high heat for 10-15 minutes till the water dries.

4. Add salt, garam masala, chopped mint leaves, lemon juice, black cumin powder and half the green coriander. Cool the mixture.

5. Fill each tomato cup with the mushroom mixture and cover with the tomato top.

Bake the stuffed tomatoes in a greased baking tray for 15 minutes.

6. For the sauce, heat oil in a pan. Sauté the cardamoms, bayleaf, onions, garlic and chopped tomatoes. Then add 2 cups water and salt and cook for about 30 minutes.

7. Strain the sauce through a fine sieve. Transfer to a saucepan and bring to a slow boil. Add cream and mace powder.

8. Pour the sauce over the baked tomatoes and sprinkle the remaining half of the green coriander before serving.

—— ❖ ——

Smooth Salt

Put a pinch of arrowroot in salt to avoid lumping.

—— ❖ ——

PUNJABI CHANA MASALA

(Bengal gram, cooked the traditional Punjabi way)

Serves: 4-5   Preparation time: 45 minutes   Cooking time: 1 hour

Ingredients

Bengal gram, whole *(chana)*,
250 gm / 1¼ cups
Water 1½ lt / 7½ cups
Bayleaf *(tej patta)* 1
Cinnamon *(dalchini)* stick 1
Butter 40 gm / 2²/₃ tbsp
Onions, chopped 100 gm / ½ cup
Garam masala (p. 6) 6 gm / 1¹/₃ tsp
Ginger *(adrak)* paste (p. 8)
10 gm / 2 tsp
Garlic *(lasan)* paste (p. 8) 10 gm / 2 tsp
Tomatoes, skinned, chopped
60 gm / 4 tbsp
Salt to taste
Green coriander *(hara dhaniya)*,
chopped 5 gm / 1 tsp

Method

1. Clean the Bengal gram, wash in water 3 or 4 times and soak for 30 minutes.

2. Boil water in a saucepan. Add the bayleaf, cinnamon stick and the drained Bengal gram; bring to a slow boil. Remove the scum from the top of the pan and simmer until the gram is completely cooked and tender. Discard the bayleaf and cinnamon sticks.

3. Heat the butter in a pan and sauté the onions till they are soft and golden. Add the garam masala, ginger-garlic pastes and sauté over medium heat for 2-3 minutes.

4. Add the tomatoes, cooked gram and salt. Cover and cook for another 2-3 minutes. Serve hot, garnished with green coriander.

KARHI

(Gram flour dumplings in tangy yoghurt curry)

Serves: 4   Preparation: 45 minutes   Cooking: 30 minutes

Ingredients

Gram flour (*besan*) 120 gm / ½ cup
Yoghurt (*dahi*) (p. 6)
360 gm / 1¾ cups
Salt to taste
Red chilli powder 5 gm / 1 tsp
Turmeric (*haldi*) powder 5 gm / 1 tsp
Soda bicarbonate *a pinch*
Carom (*ajwain*) seeds
2½ gm / ½ tsp
Green chillies, chopped 5
Groundnut oil (*moongphali tel*) + for
frying 60 ml / 4 tbsp
Potatoes, cut into rounds
150 gm / ¾ cup
Onion, cut in ¼" thick rounds
150 gm / ¾ cup

Cumin (*jeera*) seeds 2 ½ gm / ½ tsp
Mustard (*rai*) seeds 1 ½ gm / ¼ tsp
Fenugreek (*methi*) seeds 1½ gm / ¼ tsp
Red chillies, whole 4

Method

1. Whisk yoghurt, salt, red chilli powder, turmeric and half the gram flour in a bowl. Keep aside.
2. Sieve the other half of the gram flour and soda bicarbonate together; add the carom seeds and enough water to make a thick batter. Beat well.
3. Add green chillies.
4. Heat enough oil in a wok (*kadhai*) to deep fry.
5. Drop large spoonfuls of the batter in the oil to get 1½" puffy dumplings.
6. Fry till golden brown. Remove and keep aside.

7. Heat 45 ml / 3 tbsp oil in a pot (*handi*). Add the yoghurt mixture and 120 ml / 7-8 tbsp water. Bring to a boil, reduce and simmer for 8-10 minutes, stirring constantly to avoid the yoghurt from curdling.

8. Add potatoes and onions; cook till potatoes are tender.

9. Add dumplings, simmer for 35 minutes, remove and transfer to a serving bowl.

10. Heat the remaining oil (15 ml / 1 tbsp) in a small pan. Add the cumin, mustard and fenugreek seeds and sauté till they crackle. Add whole red chillies; remove from fire and pour this tempering over the hot curry.

11. Serve hot, garnished with chopped coriander and accompanied by boiled rice.

--- ❖ ---

Save More with Salt

Add a pinch of salt to the oil while frying dumplings, pakodas or koftas. You will consume less oil.

--- ❖ ---

DAL SULTANI

(Red gram seasoned with saffron)

Serves: 4-5   Preparation time: 40 minutes   Cooking time: 30 minutes

Ingredients

Red gram *(arhar dal)*
250 gm / 1 ¼ cups
Turmeric powder *(haldi) 5 gm / 1 tsp*
Salt to taste
Butter *(makhan) 50 gm / ¼ cup*
Onions, quartered *150 gm / ¾ cup*
Caraway seeds *(shahi jeera)*
5 gm / 1 tsp
Red chilli powder *10 gm / 2 tsp*
Cream *30 gm / 2 tbsp*
Saffron (soaked in cream)
1 gm / a pinch

Method

1. Wash the dal 3 or 4 times in running water and soak for half an hour in cold water.
2. In a heavy pan boil 2 lt water. Add the red gram and return to boil. Remove the scum from the top.
3. Reduce the heat. Add two-thirds of the turmeric powder. Cover and cook until the gram is completely soft. Add salt.
4. In a separate pan, heat butter on a low flame. Add onions and sauté over medium heat. Add the cumin seeds, the remaining turmeric powder and red chilli powder and stir. When the seeds begin to splutter, add the cooked gram. Cover and cook for 2-3 minutes.
5. Pour the cream-saffron mixture over the cooked gram and serve with boiled rice.

69

STUFFED POTATOES IN FENUGREEK AND SPINACH CURRY

Serves: 4   Preparation time: 45 minutes   Cooking time: 1 hour

Ingredients

Potatoes (medium, round) *1 kg*
Mint (*pudina*) leaves *45 gm / 3 tbsp*
Green coriander (*hara dhaniya*)
90 gm / 6 tbsp
Green chillies, chopped *10*
Cumin (*jeera*) seeds *2 ½ gm / ½ tsp*
Raw mango powder (*amchoor*)
5 gm / 1 tsp
Raisins (*kishmish*) *20 gm / 4 tsp*
Salt to taste
Oil + for frying *90 ml / 6 tbsp*
Turmeric (*haldi*) powder
2 ½ gm / ½ tsp
Tomatoes, chopped *80 gm / ⅓ cup*
Spinach (*palak*), chopped
400 gm / 2 cups

Fenugreek (*methi*) leaves,
chopped *105 gm / ½ cup*
Red chilli powder *10 gm / 2 tsp*
Yoghurt (*dahi*) (p. 6) *45 gm / 3 tbsp*
Garam masala (p. 6) *5 gm / 1 tsp*
Coriander (*dhaniya*) powder *5 gm / 1 tsp*
Clarified butter (*ghee*) *30 ml / 2 tbsp*

Method

1. Peel and scoop out a spoonful from the centres of the potatoes; deep fry the shells till they are crisp and golden brown.

2. Grind mint, coriander leaves, green chillies, cumin seeds, mango powder, raisins and salt with very little water to make a chutney (relish) and set aside.

3. Heat 6 tbsp oil in a wok (*kadhai*). Add turmeric powder, tomatoes, spinach and fenugreek leaves. Sauté lightly.

4. Stir in red chilli powder and salt and cook till the curry thickens. Mix in the yoghurt, garam masala, coriander powder and clarified butter.

5. Remove from heat and allow to cool. Blend to a thick purée and reheat.

6. Spoon the prepared chutney into the potatoes.

7. Place the potatoes in a shallow dish and pour the curry over them.

8. Serve hot.

❖

A Store of Mint

When mint leaves are available in plenty, dry them in the sun and add rock salt and cumin powder. Store in an airtight container and use whenever necessary.

❖

SPICED CAULIFLOWER

Serves: 4-5   Preparation time: 10 minutes   Cooking time: 45 minutes

Ingredients

Cauliflowers *(phool gobi)*, small,
whole, destemmed *5*
Oil for frying
Onions, chopped *200 gm / 1 cup*
Cashewnuts *(kaju) 100 gm / ½ cup*
Green cardamoms *(choti elaichi) 6*
Turmeric *(haldi)* powder *5 gm / 1 tsp*
Red chilli powder *10 gm / 2 tsp*
Ginger *(adrak)* paste (p. 8)
25 gm / 5 tsp
Garlic *(lasan)* paste (p. 8) *25 gm / 5 tsp*
Garam masala (p. 6) *10 gm / 2 tsp*
Yoghurt *(dahi)* (p. 6), whisked
200 gm / 1 cup
Salt to taste
Butter *30 gm / 2 tbsp*
Lemon juice *15 ml / 1 tbsp*
Mace *(javitri)* powder *3 gm / ½ tsp*

Method

1. Wash and clean the cauliflowers.
2. Heat oil in a wok (*kadhai*), deep fry each cauliflower over medium heat until almost cooked.
3. In the same oil, fry onions and cashewnuts (saving a few for garnishing). Grind to a fine paste.
4. Heat 5 tbsp oil in a pan. Add cardamoms and sauté for a few seconds. Add turmeric powder, red chilli powder, ginger-garlic pastes and garam masala and cook for 30 seconds.
5. Add onion-cashewnut paste and whisked yoghurt. Cook for 10 minutes on low heat and season with salt.
6. Arrange the fried cauliflower in a baking dish and pour the curry over each cauliflower. Bake in a moderate oven of 175 °C / 350 °F for 10 minutes.
7. Garnish with fried cashewnuts, melted butter, lemon juice and mace powder. Serve hot.

CHANA PINDI

(Chickpea curry)

Serves: 4-5   Preparation time: 3 hours 15 minutes   Cooking time: 1 hour

Ingredients

Chickpeas, whole *(kabuli chana)*
250 gm / 1¼ cups
Baking soda 5-6 gm / 1-1¹/₃ tsp
Bayleaf *(tej patta)* 1
Cardamoms, green / black *(choti / bari elaichi)* 3
Chana masala (aromatic garam masala) 5 gm / 1 tsp
Cinnamon *(dalchini)* sticks 3
Coriander *(dhaniya)* powder
5 gm / 1 tsp
Garam masala (p. 6) 5 gm / 1 tsp
Garlic *(lasan)* paste (p. 8)
10 gm / 2 tsp
Ginger *(adrak)* paste (p. 8)
10 gm / 2 tsp

Lemon juice *15 ml / 1 tbsp*
Oil *60 ml / 4 tbsp*
Red chilli powder *4 gm / ¾ tsp*
Salt for seasoning
Tea bag *1*
For garnishing:
Green chillies, whole *10*
Lemons, cut into wedges *3*
Onion rings *100 gm / ½ cup*
Tomatoes (medium), quartered *60 gm / 4 tbsp*

Method

1. Clean, wash and soak the chickpeas in water for 3 hours.
2. In a heavy pot, boil 2 lt water; add the bayleaf, cinnamon sticks, cardamoms, tea bag and chickpeas.

Bring back to boil and add baking soda. Cover and cook over low heat until the chickpeas are soft. Drain immediately. Remove the bayleaf, tea bag, cinnamon sticks and cardamoms.

3. Heat the oil in a pan over low heat. Add the ginger and garlic pastes and sauté for 30-40 seconds. Add the red chilli powder, garam masala, coriander powder, chana masala, salt and lemon juice.

4. Add the cooked chickpeas, mixing carefully.

5. Garnish with the onion rings, whole green chillies, tomatoes and lemon wedges. Serve with any Indian bread of choice (pp. 88-91).

❖

Green Chillies—High on Vitamin C

Buy green chillies when they are cheap. Clean and slit them on one side and put them in a wide-mouthed bottle or jar. Add salt and vinegar to keep the chillies fresh. They will last upto one year.

❖

MUSHROOM AND CORN BONANZA

Serves: 4-6   Preparation time: 15 minutes   Cooking time: 30 minutes

Ingredients

Mushrooms (*guchi*) 500 gm / 2½ cups
Sweet corn (*makkai*)
250 gm / 1 ¼ cups
Oil *75 ml / 5 tbsp*
Green cardamoms (*choti elaichi*) *4*
Cloves (*laung*) *3*
Mace (*javitri*) powder *a pinch*
Ginger (*adrak*) paste (p. 8)
10 gm / 2 tsp
Garlic (*lasan*) paste (p. 8) *10 gm / 2 tsp*
Onion paste (p. 8) *100 gm / ½ cup*
Cashewnut (*kaju*) paste *45 gm / 3 tbsp*
Yoghurt (*dahi*) (p. 6) *250 gm / 1¼ cups*
Green chillies, slit *4*
Salt to taste

Cream *100 ml / ½ cup*
Green coriander (*hara dhaniya*), chopped
45 gm / 3 tbsp

Method

1. Heat oil in a heavy-bottomed pan.
2. Add green cardamoms, cloves and mace powder.
When they crackle, add ginger and garlic pastes.
3. Stir-fry for a few minutes. Add onion paste and
cashewnut paste. Stir-fry for 5-6 minutes.
4. Add yoghurt, slit green chillies and salt.
5. Add mushrooms and corn; simmer for 20 minutes.
6. Stir in the cream, garnish with green coriander and
serve at once.

DUM KE BAIGAN

(Aubergines cooked on a slow fire)

Serves: 4-5   Preparation time: 10 minutes   Cooking time: 45 minutes

Ingredients

Aubergines *(baigan)*,
small, oval / round *800 gm / 20*
Oil *120 ml / ²/₃ cup*
Red chillies, whole *12*
Cumin *(jeera)* seeds *10 gm / 2 tsp*
Black pepper *(kali mirch)*
6 gm / 1 ¹/₃ tsp
Green cardamoms *(choti elaichi)* 10
Cinnamon *(dalchini)* sticks *5*
Bayleaf *(tej patta)* 1
Cloves *(laung)* 10
Malt vinegar *(sirka)* 60 ml / 4 tbsp
Onion paste (p. 8) *150 gm / ¾ cup*
Ginger *(adrak)* paste (p. 8)
40 gm / 2 ²/₃ tbsp
Turmeric *(haldi)* powder *5 gm / 1 tsp*

Garlic *(lasan)* paste (p. 8) *40 gm / 2 ²/₃ tbsp*
Salt to taste
Green coriander *(hara dhaniya)*,
chopped *15 gm / 3 tsp*

Method

1. Trim the stems of the aubergines. Slit open each aubergine crosswise, without disjoining it from the stem.

2. In a pan, heat 1 tbsp oil over medium heat. Add the red chillies, cumin seeds, black pepper, green cardamoms, cinnamon sticks, bayleaf, cloves and cumin seeds; sauté over medium heat for 5-6 minutes. Cool and grind to a fine powder.

3. Mix in vinegar to make a fine paste.

4. Heat a little oil in a pan. Fry the aubergines, a few at a time, for 5-6 minutes or until they are half cooked. Remove from the heat and keep aside.

5. In the same pan, heat the remaining oil, add the onion paste and sauté over medium heat until the paste is lightly coloured.

6. Add the ginger and garlic pastes, turmeric powder and the ground spice-paste. Stir and cook over medium heat for 4-5 minutes.

7. Add salt and $^2/_3$ cup of hot water. Cook until the water evaporates and the oil separates from the sauce.

8. Arrange the fried aubergines in the sauce. Stir very carefully, cover and cook over a low flame or in a slow oven *(dum)* for 3-4 minutes. Garnish with green coriander.

———— ❖ ————

Onion-Friendly

Peel onions under running water to avoid tears, or cut them into halves and soak them in water for a few minutes before cutting them. To skin small onions, soak them in boiling water for half a minute. Drain and cool; the skins will come off easily.

———— ❖ ————

ACHARI PANEER

(Pickled cottage cheese preserve)

Serves: 4-5   Preparation time: 15 minutes   Cooking time: 15 minutes

Method

Cottage cheese *(paneer)* (p. 8),
cubed *1 kg / 5 cups*
Mustard oil *(sarson ka tel)*
110 ml / ½ cup
Cloves *(laung)* 10
Green cardamoms *(choti elaichi)* 10
Mustard *(rai)* seeds *7 gm / 1 ½ tsp*
Fenugreek seeds *(methi dana)*
8 gm / 1²/₃ tsp
Red chillies, whole *16*
Caraway seeds *(shahi jeera)*
5 gm / 1 tsp
Onions, chopped fine *200 gm / 1 cup*
Ginger *(adrak)* paste (p. 8)
60 gm / 4 tbsp
Garlic *(lasan)* paste (p. 8)
60 gm / 4 tbsp

Red chilli powder *10 gm / 2 tsp*
Turmeric *(haldi)* powder *10 gm / 2 tsp*
Asafoetida *(hing)* a pinch
Yoghurt *(dahi)* (p. 6), whisked *300 gm / 1 ½ cups*
Salt to taste
Black pepper *(kali mirch)*, crushed
6 gm / 1 ¹/₃ tsp
Sugar *10 gm / 2 tsp*
Garlic *(lasan)* cloves 6
Lemon juice *20 ml / 4 tsp*
Green coriander *(hara dhaniya)*,
chopped *10 gm / 2 tsp*

Method

1. Heat the oil in a pan. When it starts smoking, add the cloves, cardamoms, mustard seeds, fenugreek seeds, whole red chillies and caraway seeds; stir.

2. Add the chopped onions and sauté over medium heat until brown.

3. Add the ginger and garlic pastes, red chilli powder, turmeric powder and asafoetida. Stir and cook for 3-4 minutes. Add the yoghurt, bring to a boil and simmer over low heat until the oil separates from the gravy.

4. Add the cottage cheese cubes, salt, pepper, sugar, garlic cloves and lemon juice; stir and cook for one minute.

5. Transfer to a serving dish and garnish with green coriander.

Note: This dish can be stored in a sterilized bottle in the refrigerator for 5-7 days without the green coriander.

---------- ❖ ----------

For Softer Onions . . .

Add a pinch of salt to the chopped onions while frying them for seasoning. They will turn softer quicker.

---------- ❖ ----------

VEGETABLE KORMA

(Mixed vegetables in cashewnut/almond curry)

Serves: 4-5   Preparation time: 10 minutes   Cooking time: 20 minutes

Ingredients

Carrots *(gajar)*, diced *120 gm / ²/₃ cup*
Cauliflower *(phool gobi)*, cut into
small florets *120 gm / ²/₃ cup*
French beans *(fransi bean)*
120 gm /²/₃ cup
Green peas *(mattar) 120 gm / ²/₃ cup*
Mushrooms *(guchi) 120 gm /²/₃ cup*
Potatoes, diced *120 gm / ²/₃ cup*
Onions, chopped *100 gm / ½ cup*
Oil *60 ml / 4 tbsp*
Cashewnuts / almonds *(kaju /
badam) 10*
Raisins *(kishmish) 10*
Cloves *(laung) 6*
Cinnamon *(dalchini)* sticks *3*
Bayleaf *(tej patta) 1*

Cumin *(jeera)* seeds *4 gm / ³/₄ tsp*
Green cardamoms *(choti elaichi) 8*
Ginger *(adrak)* paste (p. 8) *40 gm / 2 ²/₃ tbsp*
Garlic *(lasan)* paste (p. 8) *40 gm / 2 ²/₃ tbsp*
Green chilli paste (p. 6) *25 gm / 5 tsp*
Cashewnut *(kaju)* paste *100 gm / ½ cup*
Yoghurt *(dahi)* (p. 6), whisked *200 gm / 1 cup*
Salt to taste
White pepper *(safed mirch)* powder *3 gm /²/₃ tsp*
Cream *60 gm / 4 tbsp*
Ginger *(adrak)* juliennes (long, thin stips) *5 gm / 1 tsp*
Green coriander *(hara dhaniya)*, chopped *15 gm / 3 tsp*

Method

1. Heat a little oil in a pan. Lightly fry the cashewnuts / almonds and the raisins. Keep aside.
2. Parboil all the vegetables.

3. Heat the remaining oil. Add the cloves, cinnamon sticks, bayleaf, cumin seeds and green cardamoms and sauté until golden. Grind to a paste.

4. Add the ginger and garlic pastes, green chilli paste, cashewnut paste and the ground spices; cook until the oil separates from the gravy.

5. Add the yoghurt and cook on low heat for 5 minutes.

6. Add the parboiled vegetables, salt and white pepper. Cover and cook on low heat for 5-6 minutes.

7. Add the cream and transfer to a serving bowl. Garnish with ginger juliennes, green coriander and the fried dry fruits.

❖

Mushroom Mazaa

To keep button mushrooms fresh, put them into boiling water to which a pinch of salt has been added. Take them out after a minute, drain, cool and store in a plastic, airtight container.

❖

POTATO AND PANEER DUMPLINGS IN CURRY

Serves: 6   Preparation time: 30 minutes   Cooking time: 1 hour

Ingredients

For the dumplings:
Potatoes, boiled, mashed *3-4*
Cottage cheese (*paneer*) (p. 8), grated
500 gm / 2 ½ cups
Green coriander (*hara dhaniya*), chopped
45 gm / 3 tbsp
Mixed nuts, finely chopped *45 gm / 3 tbsp*
Turmeric (*haldi*) powder *2 gm / ½ tsp*
Asafoetida (*hing*) powder *a pinch*
Ginger (*adrak*), finely shredded *15 gm / 1 tbsp*
Green chillies, deseeded, finely chopped *1-2*
Raw mango powder (*amchoor*) *2 gm / ½ tsp*
Lemon juice *5 ml / 1 tsp*
Salt *7 gm / 1½ tsp*
Cornflour (*makkai ka atta*) *30 gm / 2 tbsp*
Oil for frying

For the curry:
Cashewnuts / almonds (*kaju / badam*),
finely chopped *40 gm / 2 ⅔ tbsp*
Ginger (*adrak*), finely chopped
15 gm / 1 tbsp
Green chillies, chopped *2*
Coriander (*dhaniya*) powder *7 gm / 1 ½ tsp*
Cumin (*jeera*) powder *5 gm / 1 tsp*
Turmeric (*haldi*) powder *2 gm / ½ tsp*
Water *250 ml / 1 ¼ cups*
Clarified butter (*ghee*) *75 ml / 5 tbsp*
Cumin (*jeera*) seeds *5 gm / 1 tsp*
Cinnamon (*dalchini*) stick (1" piece) *1*
Cloves (*laung*) *4*
Tomatoes, finely chopped
600 gm / 3 cups
Salt to taste

Method

1. For the dumplings, knead the grated cottage cheese till smooth and creamy. Add mashed potatoes, coriander, nuts, turmeric powder, asafoetida powder, ginger, green chillies, dry mango powder, lemon juice, salt and cornflour. Knead and mix thoroughly.

2. Lightly oil your hands and divide the mixture into 12 portions. Roll each portion into a ball. Place all the balls on a tray lined with plastic wrap and set aside.

3. Heat oil in a wok *(kadhai)* till it starts smoking. Slide in a few balls at a time and fry until golden brown on all sides.

4. Remove, drain excess oil on a paper towel and keep aside.

5. For the curry, process together the nuts, ginger, green chillies, coriander, cumin and turmeric powder and enough water to make a smooth paste. Set aside.

6. Moderately heat the clarified butter in a heavy-bottomed pan. Stir-fry the cumin seeds, cinnamon stick and cloves for 10-15 seconds.

7. Stir in half the tomatoes and the prepared paste. Cook until the liquid from the tomatoes dries up and the oil separates.

8. Add the remaining tomatoes, water and salt. Cover the pan and simmer for 10-15 minutes or until the curry has thickened slightly.

9. Carefully slip in the dumplings and bring the curry to a boil.

10. Spoon out the dumplings into a serving dish. Pour the curry on top and garnish with fresh coriander and cream.

11. Serve hot, accompanied by any Indian bread of choice (pp. 88-91) and green salad.

SESAME SEED AND TOMATO CHUTNEY

Serves: 4   Preparation time: 15 minutes   Cooking time: 20 minutes

Ingredients

Tomatoes, chopped *200 gm / 1 cup*
Sesame (*til*) seeds *30 gm / 2 tbsp*
Groundnut oil *(moongphali tel)*
30 ml / 2 tbsp
Onions, chopped *150 gm / ³/₄ cup*
Red chilli powder *3 gm / ¹/₂ tsp*
Turmeric (*haldi*) powder
3 gm / ¹/₂ tsp
Asafoetida (*hing*) powder *a pinch*
Black gram (*chana dal*), roasted
20 gm / 4 tsp
For the tempering:
Oil *30 ml / 2 tbsp*
Red chillies, whole *5*
Curry leaves *(meethi-neem ke patte)*
10 gm / 2 tsp
Mustard (*rai*) seeds *3 gm / ¹/₂ tsp*

Method

1. Heat groundnut oil in a pan. Add onions and sauté till light brown.

2. Stir in red chilli powder, turmeric powder, asafoetida powder and sesame seeds. Stir-fry for a few minutes.

3. Add tomatoes along with black gram and cook further for 10 minutes.

4. Remove from heat and allow to cool. Blend to make a paste and remove to a bowl.

5. For the tempering, heat oil in a pan and add red chillies, curry leaves and mustard seeds. Sauté till they crackle and remove from heat.

6. Add the prepared tempering to the chutney and serve.

MIXED PICKLE

Preparation time: 7 days   Cooking time: 20 minutes

Ingredients

Cauliflower *(phool gobi)* ½ kg
Turnips *300 gm*
Carrots *(gajar)* 300 gm
Mustard oil *(sarson ka tel)*
350 ml / 1¾ cups
Onions, puréed *100 gm / 1½ cups*
Ginger-garlic *(adrak-lasan)* paste
(p. 8) *60 gm / ¼ cup*
Sugar *200 gm / 1 cup*
Vinegar *(sirka)* 200 ml / 1 cup
Garam masala (p. 6) *25 gm / 5 tsp*
Red chilli powder *20 gm / 4 tsp*
Cumin *(jeera)* seeds *20 gm / 4 tsp*
Mustard *(rai)* seeds *20 gm / 4 tsp*
Salt to taste

Method

1. Cut the cauliflower into florets, turnips and carrots into thin slices. Dry in the sun for two days.
2. Heat mustard oil in a wok *(kadhai)*. Add onion purée and ginger-garlic paste and stir-fry for a few minutes.
3. Dissolve sugar in vinegar and keep aside.
4. Stir in the dry spices along with salt to taste and the vegetables. Cover and cook for 5-10 minutes.
5. Add the vinegar mixture to the vegetables and mix well. Remove from heat and allow to cool.
6. Transfer into a glass jar and cover with a cloth. Keep in the sun for 5 days. Serve as an accompaniment with any meal.

PUDINA PARANTHA

(Wholewheat bread flavoured with mint)

Serves: 4   Preparation time: 30 minutes   Cooking time: 10 minutes

Ingredients

Wholewheat flour (*atta*)
½ kg / 2 ½ cups
Salt *5 gm / 1 tsp*
Clarified butter (*ghee*)
120 gm / ½ cup
Water *250 ml / 1 ¼ cups*
Mint (*pudina*) leaves, dried
5 gm / 1 tsp

Method

1. Mix flour, salt and half of clarified butter; add water and knead to a smooth dough. Cover and keep aside for 30 minutes.

2. Shape the dough into a ball. Flatten into a round disc with a rolling pin. Apply the remaining clarified butter and sprinkle dried mint leaves.

3. Pleat the dough into 1 collected strip. Shape into balls and roll out into 6"-diameter pancakes.

4. Heat a griddle (*tawa*) / tandoor and cook till brown spots appear on both the sides.

Taftan

Khasta Roti

Pudina Parantha

Missi Roti

TAFTAN

(Rich, leavened, rice-flour bread)

*Serves: 4   Preparation time: 1 hour
Cooking time: 10 minutes*

Ingredients

Rice flour (*chawal ka atta*) *480 gm / 2 ½ cups*
Salt to taste, Water
Sugar *3 gm / ½ tsp*
Milk *240 ml / 1 cup*
Clarified butter *(ghee) 180 gm / ¾ cup*
Yeast *3 gm / ½ tsp*
Melon *(magaz)* seeds *10 gm / 2 tsp*
Green coriander (*hara dhaniya*),
chopped *10 gm / 2 tsp*

Method

1. Sieve flour and salt together.
2. Make a well in the flour. Add water, sugar, milk, clarified butter, yeast and melon seeds. Mix gradually and knead into a soft dough.

3. Divide into 4 equal balls and set aside for half an hour.
4. Dust lightly and roll into 3 ½" discs, ¼" thick. Sprinkle with coriander.
5. Bake in a tandoor till brown.
6. Brush with clarified butter and serve hot.

MISSI ROTI

*(Flavoured gram-flour bread cooked
in a tandoor)*

*Serves: 4   Preparation time: 30 minutes
Cooking time: 10 minutes*

Ingredients

Gram flour (*besan*) *300 gm / 1 ½ cups*
Flour (*maida*) *100 gm / ½ cup*
Green chillies, chopped *25 gm / 5 tsp*
Ginger (*adrak*), chopped *25 gm / 5 tsp*

Green coriander (*hara dhaniya*),
chopped *25 gm / 5 tsp*
Pomegranate seeds (*anardana*), *20 gm / 4 tsp*
Cumin (*jeera*) seeds *15 gm / 1 tbsp*
Onion seeds (*kalonji*) *25 gm / 5 tsp*
Salt *10 gm / 2 tsp*
Butter *100 gm / ½ cup*
Clarified butter (*ghee*) *30 gm / 2 tbsp*

Method

1. Chop green chillies, ginger and coriander finely.

2. Crush pomegranate, cumin and onion seeds with a rolling pin.

3. Mix all ingredients except butter; knead to a soft dough with water.

4. Shape into balls and roll out into 6"-diameter pancakes.

5. Cook on a griddle (*tawa*) or in a tandoor until brown on both sides.

6. Remove from fire, apply butter and serve hot.

KHASTA ROTI

(Wholewheat oven-baked bread)

Serves: 4-5   Preparation time: 25 minutes   Cooking time: 10-15 minutes

Ingredients

Wholewheat flour (*atta*) *500 gm / 2 ½ cups*
Salt to taste, Sugar *12 gm / 2 ½ tsp*
Carom (*ajwain*) seeds *15 gm / 1 tbsp*
Water *300 ml / 1 ½ cups*

Method

1. Sieve flour; add salt, sugar and carom seeds. Knead into a hard dough with water. Cover with a moist cloth and keep aside for 15 minutes.

2. Divide the dough into 10 balls. Dust and roll into 10 cm *rotis*. Prick with a fork evenly.

3. Bake the *rotis* in an oven at 175 °C / 350 °F for 8-10 minutes or till light brown in colour.

Glossary of Cooking Terms

Baste : Moisten meat, poultry or game during roasting by spooning over it, its juices.

Batter : A fluid mixture of flour, egg and milk/water used in cooking and for cooking food before frying.

Blanch : Immerse in boiling water so that the peel comes off.

Desiccate : Remove the moisture from; dry.

Marinade : A seasoned mixture of oil, vinegar, lemon juice, etc. in which meat, poultry and fish is left for some time to soften its fibres and add flavour to it.

Purée : Fruit, meat, fish, vegetables pounded, sieved or pulverised in an electric blender.

Roast : Cook in an oven or in open heat.

Sauté : Fry quickly over strong heat in fat or oil.

Simmer : Keep boiling gently on low heat.

Skewer : Fasten together pieces of food compactly on a specially designed long pin, for cooking.

Stir-fry : Fry rapidly while stirring and tossing.

Stock : Liquid produced when meat, poultry, bones, vegetables are simmered in water with herbs and flavourings for several hours; stock forms the basis of soups, stews, etc.

Whip : Beat cream, eggs, etc. to make a froth.

INDEX

ACCOMPANIMENTS

ACKNOWLEDGEMENTS

Grateful thanks to the Master Chefs at **The Intercontinental Hotel,** New Delhi,
and the **Oberoi Group of Hotels,** New Delhi, for making available their
kitchens for the preparation and photography of the dishes.

ISBN: 978-81-7436-073-0

© **This edition Roli & Janssen BV 2009**

Sixth impression
Published in India by Roli Books in arrangement with Roli & Janssen BV
M 75, Greater Kailash II Market, New Delhi-110 048, INDIA
Tel.: ++91 (011) 4068 2000, Fax: ++91 (011) 2921 7185
E-mail: info@rolibooks.com; Website: rolibooks.com

Photographs: Dheeraj Paul

Printed in India